10

MASTER
REWARDS

for

Sitting Daily in the
Presence of God

MIKE
SMALLEY

10 Master Rewards
For Sitting Daily in The Presence of God

ISBN: **0-9786376-6-6**

Cover Design: Roark Creative: ***www.roarkcreative.com***

HONOR ROLL

The following individuals made the printing of this book possible. I encourage all who are benefited by this book to call their names in prayer.

TABLE OF CONTENTS

INTRODUCTION

It happened in Honolulu, Hawaii.

Sitting in a television studio where I was to teach for 2 hours.

Waiting quietly alone, the revelation came:

God is more "reward conscious" than we are "God conscious!"

God thinks about "reward", more than we think about Him!

Children in every country play the game hide and seek.

We have an inner persuasion from childhood, even in our play time, there is a reward for seeking out the unseen. . . the overlooked. . . the undiscovered.

For months God's been stirring me on the subject of "divine reward."

He is more reward oriented than any of us have ever realized.

God's business *is* the reward business. The universe operates under the law of divine reward.

Man decides.

God rewards.

"But without faith it is impossible to please Him: for he that cometh to God must believe that He is, and that He is a rewarder of them that diligently seek Him." (Heb 11:6)

According to this verse, I don't have to understand God's love to approach Him.

I don't have to acknowledge His power on the earth.

I don't even have to have a revelation of His holiness.

However, in order to pleasure Him, I MUST, in faith, believe He exists and that

He is a **rewarder** of those who diligently seek Him.

Every commandment in Scripture is linked to a promised reward if we obey.

Jeremiah 33:3 "Call unto me. . ."

Many times in our busyness, our inward reply is, "Not now, Lord. I have so much to do."

Why many times in our hectic schedules do we ignore the drawing of the Holy Spirit to pray?

Answer:

Because we remain unpersuaded the reward of calling on Him is greater than the satisfaction of completing our daily tasks.

Look again at the promised reward: "Call unto me, **and I will answer thee, and show thee great and mighty things, which thou knowest not.**"

Scripture shares with us numerous rewards for entering daily into the

Presence of God.

"Glory and honor are in His presence. Strength and gladness are in His place."
(1 Chron. 16:27)

The following pages will introduce you to *10 Master Rewards* you simply can't afford to live without.

Wisdom reaches for a life of reward.

My prayer is the seasons of your life will forever change as you learn to taste the rewards of *Sitting Daily in the Presence Of God.*

REWARD 1

Public Reward

It happened alone in my Secret Place!

Six AM.

My wife was sleeping.

My children were still in bed.

No sunlight had yet graced the sky. The phone was wonderfully silent. No emails seemed important.

I was alone in my Secret Place, the private prayer room in my home, where I meet with the Holy Spirit. Suddenly, exploding like a thousand suns, He brought to my mind a golden reward Jesus Himself promised. I had read it many times . . . but had *long* forgotten it.

"But thou, when thou prayest, enter

into thy closet, and when thou hast shut thy door, pray to thy father which is in secret; And thy father which seeth in secret **shall reward thee openly"**.

(Matt 6:6)

Most seek the rewards of life in the open market place, and retreat at night to their homes dreading to be alone. . . unseen and isolated.

Jesus taught the opposite.

The person who spends "alone time" *with God* will be rewarded in the open market place!

There is nothing wrong with corporate public prayer. . . the habit of praying with a group of believers.

Nations have been shaken and changed at every level of society when the people of God prayed corporately.

There is a great current of strength, energy and blessing released when you join with other Christians *in unity* for public prayer.

As powerful and necessary as corporate

prayer is, it remains a holy activity occurring before human eyes. *It simply contains a different reward.*

Praying alone daily requires a much deeper commitment. A greater hunger. . . a greater passion.

Why?

The corporate strength present in public meetings is not available to draw from.

Pursuing God without the benefit of other's present. . . other's faith. . . other's strength. . . requires a greater level of faith.

A greater level of *reaching*.

The Holy Spirit recognized this before time began and inserted a divine reward in the prayer equation to motivate you to reach . . . and to guarantee your reaching would never be in vain!

". . . And your father which sees in secret *shall reward you openly*".
(Matt 6:6)

Every time you choose to enter a place no one sees but you and the Holy Spirit, He schedules a public reward that everyone around you sees!

Master the habit of visualizing this promise being released toward your life.

When Jesus promised praying in secret would authorize a public reward . . .He meant just that . . . A PUBLIC reward. *One your friends. . . and. . . your enemies* will be forced to acknowledge.

When you enter the presence of God *alone,* regardless of your current faith level. . . or feelings. . . your Heavenly Father documents your obedience and schedules a public reward!

God's reward system works every time when accurately applied. . . in every country. . .in every economy. . . and for every believer.

Only time alone in His presence authorizes the Holy Spirit to schedule *this kind of* public reward.

Each day I refuse to meet alone with Him is a day I tie the hand of God. . . a day He is unable to release toward me His river of reward.

Every 24 hours I live without entering His presence **alone**, I authorize scheduled times of loss. . . a future day *without* Divine Reward.

His precious promise of "public reward" always hinges on my pursuing Him... alone.

Reach *today.*

Reach *often.*

Reach *with passion.*

Reach *with expectation.*

Reach *alone.*

Public Reward. . . .it's one of the many *Master Rewards* to *Sitting Daily in the Presence of God.*

REWARD 2
National Revival

Your prayers have been deciding the plans of God!

"If my people, which are called by my name, shall humble themselves, and pray, and seek my face, and turn from their wicked ways; then will I hear from heaven and will forgive their sin, and will heal their land."

(2 Chron. 7:14)

Your nation's future is not being decided by its current leaders, threat of terrorism or its economy.

The present conditions and future of any nation are always being decided by the born again believers living within that nation!

As the late Leonard Ravenhill said, "As

the church goes, so goes the world."

The opposite is never true.

God has always lets His people decide what kind of world they live in.

(Dt. 28, Lev. 26)

It is clear today the church in the Western world is in need of one of the *Master Rewards for Sitting Daily in the Presence of God:* the Reward of National Revival.

The outward appearance of revival may look different in each generation, but the inward result is the same. . . a new passion for God to consume all of us!

Revival is one of the master rewards God gives to a people, individual church and nation for entering His Presence and obeying 2 Chronicles 7:14.

It's the reward that changes EVERYTHING!

Revival births a hatred for indwelling sin.

Revival produces an intense hunger for

the presence and approval of God.

Revival is never birthed in a day.

Revival never occurs without great cost.

Revival never stays within the walls of a local church.

Revival never fails to change the moral climate of a city. . . or a nation.

God promised in 2 Chronicles 7:14 the current generation of believers present in any society could bring the reward of revival to their nation!

Everything Hinges On "IF"

"If my people. . ."

What's Holding Back The Reward Of National Revival?

In general, our laziness in chasing after God.

Our "new approaches" do not seem

to be winning more people to Christ but merely encouraging already established Christians to *move* from one church to another.

Pastors who have given their lives to help their people regularly hear, "God is leading us to another church. It's nothing personal, but they have more programs for our family."

This is not the church's fault, but rather a *revealer* of the current mindset of the average Western Christian who equates size with the presence of God. *We have little discernment—and even less desperation.*

While we are angry and leaving "our church" because someone hurt our feelings, across town is a mosque where radical Muslims are training their children to be suicide bombers.

I have witnessed our fascination with large crowds and our assumption the ability to pack more and more people in a building automatically equals the approval of God on what we are doing and what we are teaching.

Yet, I am witnessing the fastest moving away from the Holy Spirit I have seen in my lifetime of 25 years of preaching.

Crowds in and of themselves are not a sign of the approval or disapproval of God.

Has it occurred to us Disney World has no problem attracting a crowd?

While there are pockets of revival throughout the earth, the church in the Western world is largely ineffective in impacting their communities for Christ.

One look into the average local church (large or small) reveals:

- Families are in crisis.

- Severe depression is becoming more common.

- In-depth Bible knowledge is at an all time low.

- Passion for more than one service a week is almost nonexistent.

More Not Less

The Bible never requires us to meet on any particular week night or time of day and there is nothing in Scripture commanding Sunday night church services.

However, the Bible does COMMAND believers to gather together *more, not less* as they see "the Day" (of the Lord) approaching.

"Not forsaking the assembling of ourselves together, as the manner of some is; but exhorting one another: and so much the more, as ye see the day approaching."

(Heb 10:25)

When the New Testament command is clearly to meet corporately with believers more and more as the Day of the Lord's judgment approaches, why are we canceling services instead of adding them?

Canceling services or the number of times Christians gather together– does not nurture a climate for revival, but actually sends the message to a watching world there is no crisis on the earth and God's presence and the teaching of His Word are not interesting enough to reach for more than one hour a week!

Are we guilty as leaders today of accommodating people's laziness after God?

Meanwhile, drugs addicts remain desperate. Teenage prostitutes live in hopelessness. Suicide rates continue to climb, and many Christians live in a continual battle for their mind while swimming in a sea of despair.

People's pain matters.

Is our prayerlessness the loudest silence in God's ears?

Many in the church have exchanged intercession for worship. We gather for hours to hear the best musicians sing, but recoil at the idea of a 2 hour prayer meeting on Friday night.

Prayer meetings remain the lowest attended gatherings at the average church, while concerts and congregational meals remain the most attended functions.

While revival is not an evangelist coming in for Sunday through Wednesday church services, the tradition of focusing God's people on special seasons of internal examination, confession, repentance, and the presence of God have been the means, historically, for setting in motion the Great Awakenings of the past.

We live in a very demonized world and the church in many parts of the earth (particularly in the West) is asleep or apathetically awake!

It's not too late! God still responds to desperation and humilty.

Good will cannot birth that encounter.

Good intentions don't launch revival.

A dismay, anger or sorrow over national tragedies does not produce the reward of revival.

Revival is not a mystery . . . and revival is never a miracle.

Revival is simply a process of Sowing the right Seed and receiving the Promised Harvest.

God is roaming the earth looking for someone's life, someone's city and someone's nation to shower with the reward of revival.

The Reward of National Revival.

God is daring you to take Him up on it!

REWARD 3
Divine Justice

This is the most undiscovered Divine Reward!

Satan knows Christians don't have to sin to bring chaos to the earth.

Satan understands when a Christian ceases to enter into the Presence of God *daily*, evil will automatically have an advantage over good.

Without *His presence*, there is no Divine Justice imparted within us.

Heaven's Most Unusual Prayer Request

Revelation 6 records one of the most revealing truths in Scripture. Perhaps the most unusual gathering in Heaven.

There is no record of their worship.

There is no record of their singing or dancing.

No mention of their falling at the feet of Jesus.

Their one request was simple:

REVENGE.

"And when He had opened the fifth seal, I saw under the altar the souls of them that were slain for the Word of God, and for the testimony for which they held: And they cried with a loud voice, saying, How long, O Lord, holy and true, dost thou not judge and avenge our blood on them that dwell on the earth?

(Rev. 6: 9-10)

This passage deserves serious meditation.

Their first prayer request in heaven (the only place it is impossible to have a wrong desire) was for God to kill the people who had murdered them!

Essentially, their cry to Jesus was: "We're in heaven now because people still living on the earth murdered us. How long before you avenge our deaths? We want revenge!"

Heaven. . . the ultimate dwelling place of God and *His presence*. . . birthed in them a passion for His justice on the earth.

Jesus never rebuked them for their request.

His reaction documented they were not wrong in what they were asking.

When I Enter God's Presence, He Imparts To Me His Passion For Divine Justice.

This explains the "unusual" prayer request of these martyred believers in Heaven. The moment they entered the presence of God, His sense of Divine Justice exploded in them with such strength they were not captivated by what was occurring in Heaven, but consumed by what was *not happening* on the earth.

The longer a believer is out of the presence of God, the less he will be concerned about God's justice being carried out on the earth.

When the church loses her sense of divine justice, evil dominates the earth.

When evil dominates, it is impossible for you and your loved ones not to be effected.

Each day a Christian fails to enter the presence of God is a day the Holy Spirit's reward of divine justice is absent from their life. When God's passion is not transferred into you daily, your sin nature gains strength.

How Important Is Justice To God?

He hath showed thee, O man, what is good; and what doth the Lord require of thee, but to do justly, and to love mercy, and to walk humbly with thy God.

(Micah 6:8)

Consider David

David understood the key to entering God's presence. . .*singing.*

". . . Come before His presence with singing." (Ps 100:2b)

The Psalmist David unlocked a divine law while spending weeks alone tending sheep. *His singing* brought him into the presence of God, which deposited within Him a passion for Divine Justice.

There is no Biblical account of any other Israelite at that time who entered God's Presence through singing.

Since the reward of Divine Justice dwelt in David, it is no shock he is the only Israelite, when confronted with Goliath, who defiantly asked, *"...who is this uncircumcised Philistine, that he should defy the armies of the living God?"*

(I Sam 17:26b)

Jesus And The Money Changers

Jesus had 12 disciples who continually heard Him teach. However, He is the only one who privately entered God's presence daily. Thus, His disciples walked through the temple regularly and remained undisturbed.

Not Jesus.

The disciples reacted with passive contentment.

Jesus reacted by making a whip! "When He had made a whip of cords, He drove them all out of the temple. . ."

(John 2:15a NKJV)

Jesus was showcasing Divine Justice. This wasn't some failure of Jesus he had to repent of. *He knew no sin.* He was right to exercise His Father's Divine Justice in a God honoring way.

If your sense of the justice of God is not stirred, birthed, and maintained in the presence of God, you will live to see the day sin and militant evil no longer concern you.

Divine Justice protects.

Divine Justice is a defense against evil.

Divine Justice is Heaven's equalizer on the earth.

Divine Justice reestablishes Divine order in the universe.

Divine Justice is not a gift. . . *It's a Reward for Sitting Daily in the Presence of God.*

REWARD 4

His Anointing

There is no substitute for the anointing of the Holy Spirit!

". . . and the yoke shall be destroyed because of the anointing"

(Is. 10:27)

Many volumes have been written on "the anointing."

The majesty & mystery of it have often kept us from understanding how it works in our day to day lives.

The anointing is a "divine enablement" to obey the instructions of God and to live the Christian life without being stained by the wickedness around you.

Your willpower will never be enough.

Your personality will affect men's minds.

His anointing will transform their heart.

Never attempt in the natural what can only be accomplished through the anointing.

Even Jesus refused to enter His public ministry until He was visited by the Holy Spirit.

"And Jesus, when he was baptized, went up straightway out of the water: and, lo, the heavens were opened unto him, and he saw the Spirit of God descending like a dove, and lighting upon him."
(Mat 3:16)

A saved man is not always an anointed man.

An experience with God in the past does not guarantee you are anointed for your future.

Many born again Christians never seek the reward of His anointing on their life or for their daily tasks.

They are going to Heaven, but are usually failing on the earth.

Never confuse a visitation from God in the past with approval for your present.

God welcomes you to return on a continual basis to His presence. *And He, in turn, continually rewards your passion with His anointing.*

Jesus understood the vital need for the Holy Spirit's divine enablement and commanded His disciples, "And, behold, I send the promise of my Father upon you: but tarry ye in the city of Jerusalem, until ye be endued with power from on high."

(Luke 24:49)

Men who had walked physically with Jesus for three and a half years were unqualified to take His message to the earth without the enablement of the Holy Spirit. How much more are we, 2000 years from the cross, in need of this precious promised reward of the Father?

"But ye shall receive power, after that the Holy Ghost is come upon you: and ye shall be witnesses unto me both in Jerusalem, and in all Judaea, and in Samaria, and unto the uttermost part of the earth."

(Acts 1:8)

What was necessary for Peter, James and John is even more necessary for you and I.

Satan robs. . . *God rewards*.

Enter His presence today with expectation and exit with a new anointing.

His Anointing. . . It's the irreplaceable *Reward For Sitting Daily In The Presence Of God*.

REWARD 5
Answers

Nobody talks more than God!

Nothing is more agitating to a Christian who wants to please God than not knowing what God wants for their life.

One of the *Master Rewards for Sitting Daily in the Presence of God* is His voice becomes magnified... drowning out the human voices that often dominate our decision making.

Moses heard God talk at the burning bush.

Joseph heard from God in his dreams.

Saul abandoned a lifetime of human training after a 10 second conversation with Jesus on the road to Damascus.

The Night That Changed Everything

I had a very real encounter with the Holy Spirit when I was 14 years of age that left a permanent mark on my life. I had entered God's presence twice a day for several days at a youth camp in Texas.

In *His presence* a major life question was permanently answered. "What does God want me to do with my future?" The answer became undeniably clear. *I was to spend the rest of my life in full time preaching ministry.*

In the years since that encounter, I have doubted my salvation many times, but never my call to the ministry. It was that strong. . . it was that clear. It was my reward for setting aside one week in His presence.

Questions Still Unanswered

Though my new call into full time ministry was unshakably clear, a thousand questions about that calling remained unanswered for several years.

I didn't know whether I was going to be a youth minister, missionary, pastor, or evangelist. I just knew I'd spend the rest of my life preaching. So, I obeyed what I knew, stayed in His presence and He rewarded me later with the answers I needed to complete my life assignment.

The Experience of John

In Revelation chapter one, the Holy Spirit documents for us the process by which He answered the questions of the Apostle John.

John was the only one of Jesus' disciples who died of natural causes. However, the last few years of John's life, he was in prison on the isle of Patmos.

After years of persecution for preaching the Gospel (including being boiled in oil), it would be understandable from the human perspective, for John to be passive about pursuing God.

That however, was NOT the attitude or passion of John. He viewed his deliverance from death in boiling oil as another sign of the approval and anointing of God for his future. He continued to preach well into his 90s and probably thought after being banished to the isle of Patmos his ministry was over.

He was wrong.

John reveals to us a Master Secret to tapping into God's will:

When You're In The Pain Of A Major Crisis, Expect The Reward Of Answers While Sitting In The Presence Of God.

"I was in the Spirit on the Lord's day, and heard behind me a great voice, as of a trumpet. . ."

(Rev 1:10)

Many years ago, Dr. Mike Brown presented to our college class these three powerful truths from Revelation, chapter one.

3 Harvests From The Seed Of Pursuit

1. A New Vision Of Jesus.

John had traveled physically with

Jesus for 3 and half years. He knew what Jesus looked like. Yet John's reaction in Revelation, chapter one, was not one of a man seeing an old and dear friend, but the reaction of a man consumed by a "God moment."

"Then I turned to see the voice that spoke with me. And having turned I saw seven golden lampstands, and in the midst of the seven lampstands One like the Son of Man, clothed with a garment down to the feet and girded about the chest with a golden band. His head and hair were white like wool, as white as snow, and His eyes like a flame of fire; His feet were like fine brass, as if refined in a furnace, and His voice as the sound of many waters; He had in His right hand seven stars, out of His mouth went a sharp two-edged sword, and His countenance was like the sun shining in its strength. And when I saw Him, I fell at His feet as dead. But He laid His right hand on me, saying to me, "Do not be afraid; I am the First and the Last. I am He who lives, and was dead, and behold, I am alive forevermore. Amen. And I have the keys of Hades and of Death."

(Rev 1:12-18 NKJV)

2. A New Vision of His Bride.

". . . the seven candlesticks which thou sawest are the seven churches."

(Rev1: 20b)

When you enter God's presence, not only will He magnify your revelation of Himself, but He will always showcase what He's in love *with*.

Everything God presently does on the earth, He does through His church. You will never receive a new revelation of Jesus without the Holy Spirit also revealing to you a new view of His bride.

3. A New Vision Of Your Life Assignment.

"**Write** the things which thou hast seen, and the things which are, and the things which shall be hereafter."

(Rev 1:19)

When John chose to enter the presence of God, he received the reward of answers. He was not to die. He was to write the last book of the Bible! John's obedience to this new and last assignment produced for the earth The Book of Revelation.

No Respecter of Persons

Because God is no respecter of persons, the same pattern that worked for John will work for you! When you sit daily in the presence of God, a divine exchange occurs.

God's plans are revealed to your mind and spirit.

Questions about what's next for your life become clear.

The battle plan emerges.

Clarity concerning your life assignment is exhilarating, liberating, and magnetic— Pursue it now! It's one of the *Master Rewards for Sitting Daily in the Presence of God!*

REWARD 6

Supernatural Joy

Happiness can always be manufactured.

The absence of joy is impossible to hide!

Joy is always a Divine Reward.

". . . in thy presence is fullness of joy; at thy right hand are pleasures forevermore."

(Psalms 16:11)

Your level of joy will always be proportionate to your time *alone* in *His presence.*

Failure to enter God's presence alone on a daily basis, I believe, is one of the major reasons for the growing number of Christians being medically treated for depression.

The Baby John the Baptist

The Bible gives us amazing insight into the ability for even a baby in its mother's womb to experience the presence of God. Scripture records the story of Mary traveling while 3 months pregnant with Jesus to meet her cousin Elizabeth who was 6 months pregnant with John the Baptist. Luke 1:44 describes the reaction of John the Baptist when he heard Mary's voice "For, lo, as soon as the voice of thy salutation sounded in mine ears, the babe leaped in my womb for joy."

How could a 6 month old baby, unable to walk or talk, recognize the voice of an aunt he'd never met?

How could a 6 month old undeveloped mind express joy? It can't.

Joy is a function of your spirit, never your mind.

"But the fruit of the Spirit is . . . joy . . ." (Gal. 5:22a)

Walking The Talk

This truth was lived out in front of me days after attending the funeral of a 43 year old man who died in an automobile accident.

The following Sunday, I was at the church the family attended. The people sang the chorus, *"I'm trading my sorrows... I'm trading my pain. I'm laying them again **for the joy of the Lord."*** I looked at his recent widow to see what her countenance might be. Her head was lifted back, her eyes were wide open and both hands were as high as she could lift them. She was singing those words with all of her heart. I said, "God, she knows something about the joy of the Lord today nobody else here knows."

Joy is a divine enablement to move with peace and a cheerful countenance through the painful, dark seasons of life.

This godly lady was not ignoring her grief or being irreverent to her husband. She was simply walking out the truth of Neh 8:10 ". . . the joy of the LORD is your strength."

Always discern the current level of joy in your life.

Joy is never absent without a reason.

If you have less joy today than in previous seasons, inventory your life in the presence of God.

What's happened?

What's departed?

What's changed?

What task has God prompted you to do that you have ignored? Who have you allowed in your inner circle that has not earned access? *Wrong people always drain your joy.*

Stay consumed with fulfilling your life assignment.

Remain focused on hearing *His voice* and *instantly* obeying.

8 Facts about Joy

1. God Is The Source Of Our Joy.
". . . in thy presence is fulness of joy; at thy right hand there are pleasures for evermore."

(Ps 16:11)

2. It Is Possible To Always Have Joy. "These things have I spoken unto you, that my joy might remain in you, and that your joy might be full."

(John 15:11)

3. Joy Is One Of The Descriptions The Bible Gives For The Kingdom Of God. "For the kingdom of God is not meat and drink; but righteousness, and peace, and joy in the Holy Ghost."

(Rom 14:17)

4. Joy Occurs In Heaven As Well As On The Earth. "I say unto you, that likewise joy shall be in heaven over one sinner that repenteth, more than over ninety and nine just persons, which need no repentance."

(Luke 15:7)

5. Joy That Is Lost Can Be Restored.
"Restore unto me the joy of thy salvation. . ."

(Ps 51:12b)

6. Present Sorrow Cannot Prevent Future Joy. "They that sow in tears shall reap in joy."

(Ps 126:5)

7. Joy Can Last Forever. "And the ransomed of the Lord shall return, and come to Zion with songs and everlasting joy upon their heads: they shall obtain joy and gladness, and sorrow and sighing shall flee away."

(Is 35:10)

8. True Joy Is Difficult To Conceal.
". . .and all the sons of God shouted for joy..."

(Job 38:7b)

Ask the Holy Spirit today to plant within you a new passion to enter His presence daily. You won't leave like you came. He is always willing to plant the seed of joy into the soil of an obedient seeker.

Your future is too precious, your mind too complex, and your emotions too fragile, to live life without the daily impartation of the joy of the Lord.

An old song describing joy says it this way, "The world didn't give it and the world can't take it away."

Happiness is temporal.

Joy is eternal.

Pursue it. Reach for it. Keep it.

Supernatural Joy. . . It's one of the *10 Master Rewards For Sitting Daily In The Presence Of God.*

Natural sleep will never produce peace of mind.

Exodus 33:14 is worth memorizing. "And he said, my presence shall go with thee, and I will give thee rest."

(Ex 33:14)

The seventh master reward for *Sitting Daily in the Presence of God* is an impartation of divine Supernatural Rest.

There is no earthly substitute for it!

The Bible says in John 10:10 "The thief cometh not, but for to steal, and to kill, and to destroy: I am come that they might have life, and that they might have it more abundantly."

Satan delights in the opportunity to

continually attack the believers mind with doubt. . . unbelief. . . and *fear*.

Satan is more patient than any Christian on the earth.

He will gladly plant seeds of destruction in your present, even if it means a harvest of destruction, devastation and loss occurs years . . . even decades later.

In the current world in which we live, suicide, demon possession, demon oppression, and mental and emotional depression are at an all time high.

Scripture forewarned this would occur in the last days.

"This know also, that in the last days perilous times shall come."

(2 Tim 3:1)

The Demoniac

The demon possessed man in Mark 5 was not in need of physical healing. There no mention in Scripture he had an illness or physical problems. However, his mind was completely dominated by the legion of demons that possessed him. In short, he was a mad man.

He cut himself.

He lived alone.

He ran among the tombs completely naked.

When this man entered the presence of Jesus, the Son of God cast the demons out. He did not heal his body. . . *He healed his mind.*

10 Facts About Rest

1. **Where You Seek Rest Determines If You Find It.** "Come unto **Me**. . . and I will give you rest."

   (Matt 11:28)

2. **Holidays And Vacations Will Not Silence The Pain Of A Broken Spirit.**

3. **Divine Rest Must Be Given Not Achieved.** "Come unto Me, all ye that labour and are heavy laden, and I will give you rest."

   (Matt 11:28)

4. Satan Strategizes Regularly To Prevent God's People From Entering And Abiding In Divine Rest. ". . . then the devil comes and takes away the word out of their hearts, lest they should believe and be saved" (Luke 8:12).

5. God Can Withhold Rest Based On Our Behavior. "So I sware in my wrath, they shall not enter into my rest."

(Heb 3:11)

6. Supernatural Rest Is Available To All Of God's People. "There remaineth therefore a rest to the people of God."

(Heb 4:9)

7. You Can Decide To Leave The Place Of Supernatural Rest. "Return unto thy rest, O my soul; for the LORD hath dealt bountifully with thee."

(Ps 116:7)

8. Friends, Family And Even Ministers Are Incapable Of Providing You Supernatural Rest. "For if Joshua had given them rest, then He would not afterward have spoken of another day."

(Heb 4:8 NKJV)

9. Supernatural Rest Births Supernatural Deliverance. "For thus saith the Lord GOD, the Holy One of Isreal; In returning and rest shall ye be saved. . ."

(Is 30:15a)

10. Asking The Right Questions Leads To Rest. ". . . ask for the old paths, where is the good way, and walk therein, and ye shall find rest for your souls. . ." (Jer 6:16b)

Mastering the daily habit of removing yourself from scheduled tasks to meet alone with God will produce great rest.

As you enter God's presence daily, enter with expectation. . . of **DIVINE REWARD.**

(For help in launching your prayer life, you'll love my book *How To Jumpstart Your Prayer Life.*)

I thank God for friends, counselors and those in the medical profession. But there is no substitute for. . . **His rest** imparted in. . . **His presence.**

Fears *fade*.

Doubts *disappear*.

Depression *dissolves*.

Weakness *withers*.

His presence produces Supernatural Rest. It's one of the *Master Rewards For Sitting Daily In The Presence Of God.*

REWARD 8

The Reward of Divine Partnership

God partners with those who pursue Him!

"Draw near to God and He will draw near to you."

(James 4:8a NKJV)

Zaccheus had the privilege of spending a private evening with Jesus for one reason:

Pursuit.

"And when Jesus came to the place, he looked up, and saw him, and said unto him, Zacchaeus, make haste, and come down; for today I must abide at thy house."

(Luke 19:5)

Nicodemus entered the presence of

Jesus at night and was the first human on the earth to hear . . . **John 3:16!**

Dr. Mike Murdock taught me one of the greatest revelations about God I've ever had:

"God does not respond to pain. . . He does not respond to needs."

I have learned He responds to being reached for in the midst of pain. He reacts to our faith and expectation in the middle of a need.

". . .and that He is a rewarder of them that diligently seek Him."

(Heb 11:6b)

Many on the earth have urgent needs.

What is the "divine magnet" that draws God to become involved and partner with us in our crisis?

Entering His presence and reaching.

"If, when evil cometh upon us, as the sword, judgment, or pestilence, or famine, we stand before this house, and in thy presence ... and cry unto thee in our

affliction, then thou wilt hear and help."
(2 Chron 20:9)

When did God say He will hear and help? When they are surrounded by evil and they cry unto Him in their pain.

Where were they at?

In His presence.

Not at the feet of scorners.

Never in the company of doubters.

But when they had gone into His presence, God said, "I'm going to listen." And when God listens, God helps. Acts 3:19 says "repent ye therefore, and be converted…" Why? "That your sins may be blotted out, when the times of refreshing shall come from the presence of the Lord."

Healing

The Bible tells a story of a woman who hemorrhaged for 12 years. Medically speaking, her continued loss of blood for over a decade had left her anemic, weak and unable to function in society.

Her reaching for the best physicians available documents her wisdom.

However, the best of what man has to offer will often miserably fail to bring us the miracle we desperately need.

In short, all men need God.

In the midst of our pain and trials, God will always Sow a Seed of invitation. Our reaction to that invitation determines God's next reaction to us.

"Hey lady, Jesus of Nazareth is about to walk down your street."

She could have easily sneered, "If He's really God's son, He knows where I am. Let Him come to me."

Her decision to pursue her miracle documents the draining of strength from her body had not stripped her of the inner persuasion that her pain was not permanent.

Angels never visited her.

Leaders had no counsel to offer.

There were no past examples of miracles from touching the clothes of prophets.

Reachers refuse to let the inexperience of others forecast the outcome of their future miracles.

Consider her faith declaration:

"For she said within herself, If I may but touch his garment, I shall be whole."
(Matt 9:21)

Notice Jesus never responded to her pain or her need. He had lived on the earth the entire 12 years she had suffered.

She was healed the day **she decided she would be.**

She was healed the day *she reached.*

She was healed the day she entered the presence of the Healer.

Her reward?

He partnered with her faith. . . and the bleeding stopped!

Deliverance

The demon possessed man in Mark 5 was not delivered merely because of Jesus compassion. Hundreds remained demon possessed during Jesus time on the earth.

What made this man different from others tormented by satanic foes?

"When he saw Jesus from afar, he ran and worshipped Him."
(Mark 5:6 NKJV)

Jesus partnered with the man's future when he entered His presence.

His need did not birth his deliverance. The place where he lived did not birth his deliverance... **his decision to place himself at the feet of Jesus did**.

Nathanael

One of my favorite of Jesus' 12 disciples is Nathanael. His future in eternity is described in Matthew 19:28 (NKJV):

"...you who have followed Me will also sit on twelve thrones, judging the twelve tribes of Israel."

God often speaks the loudest through a human voice He has placed near us.

Our reaction to that voice often brings us into the next glorious season of our future.

Always discern and evaluate the conversations of those presently in your life.

Consider Phillip's conversation with Nathanael:

"And Nathanael said unto him, Can there any good thing come out of Nazareth? Philip saith unto him, Come and see."
(John 1:46)

Nathanael's willingness to risk disappointment brought him into the presence of Jesus.

His reaching was forever rewarded.

Have you asked God to be your partner in every area of life?

Desire for God's involvement does not guarantee God's participation.

God views entering His presence daily as reaching.

Reaching births Divine Partnership.

It's one of the *10 Master Rewards for Sitting Daily in the Presence of God.*

REWARD 9
The Mantle of Wisdom

There is no substitute for the wisdom of God!

"For the Lord giveth wisdom: out of his mouth cometh knowledge and understanding."

(Prov 2:6)

If the body of Christ pursued wisdom as passionately as she pursues miracles, we would see more miracles and less tragedy.

"If any of you lack wisdom, let him ask of God, that giveth to all men liberally and upbraideth not; and it shall be given to him."

(James 1:5)

14 Scriptural Rewards Of Wisdom

1. Profit.
"For the merchandise of it is better than the merchandise of silver, and the gain thereof than fine gold."
(Proverbs 3:14)

2. Wisdom's Worth Is Greater Than Anything Else You Desire. "...and all the things thou canst desire are not to be compared unto her."
(Proverbs 3:15b)

3. Longevity.
"Length of days is in her right hand..."
(Proverbs 3:16a)

4. Riches And Honor.
"...and in her left hand riches and honour."
(Proverbs 3:16b)

5. Pleasantness.
"Her ways are ways of pleasantness..."
(Proverbs 3:17a)

6. Peace.
"...and all her paths are peace."
(Proverbs 3:17b)

7. Source of Life.
"She is a tree of life to them that lay hold upon her..."

(Proverbs 3:18a)

8. Happiness.
"...and happy is every one that retaineth her."

(Proverbs 3:18b)

9. Protection.
"For wisdom is a defense. . ."

(Ecc 7:12a)

10. Wisdom Produces Stability. "And wisdom and knowledge shall be the stability of thy times. . ."

(Is 33:6a)

11. God Marvels When He Sees No Wisdom. "...Is wisdom no more in Teman? Is counsel perished from the prudent? Is their wisdom vanished?"

(Jer 49:7b)

12. Security.
"But whoever listens to me will dwell safely, And will be secure, without fear of evil."

(Prov 1: 33 NKJV)

13.Wisdom Is Better Than Strength.
"Then said I, Wisdom is better than strength. . ."

(Ecc 9:16a)

14.Wisdom Reveals Secrets. "He giveth wisdom unto the wise, and knowledge to them that know understanding: He revealeth the deep and secret things: He knoweth what is in the darkness and the light dwelleth with him."

(Dan 2:21b-22)

"Every Problem In Your Life Is A Wisdom Problem."
-Dr. Mike Murdock

I will never forget hearing this revelation for the first time. There is no such thing as a money problem. . . marriage problem. . . or any other problem.

Every problem is simply a wisdom problem.

"My people are destroyed for lack of knowledge."

(Hosea 4:6a)

There are many parts to the wisdom equation.

You must pursue mentors. . . you must study . . . read and do everything in your power to gain understanding.

"Wisdom is the principal thing; therefore get wisdom: and with all thy getting get understanding."

(Prov. 4:7)

Entering the presence of God daily is the most important part of the wisdom equation.

God never rewards pursuit with ignorance. His words. . . His instructions...His rebukes. . . His compliments. . . always impart Wisdom.

Document your uniqueness on the earth. Become consumed with Wisdom. *Search for it first—in His presence.*

Wisdom...*It's one of the Master Rewards For Sitting Daily In The Presence Of God.*

REWARD 10

Divine Promotion

The presence of God births time sensitive opportunities so God can thrust you into the future you've always dreamed of!

A man once sat in the presence of Jesus.

He was given a **simple instruction**. . . "Arise, and take up thy bed, and walk."
(Mark 2:9b)

Jesus words were "time sensitive."

Every instruction from God has an expiration date.

Every promise. . .

Every blessing. . .

Every *reward.*

God is consumed with increase. He reacts swiftly to anything that refuses to grow. . . including fig trees. "And when he saw a fig tree in the way, he came to it, and found nothing theron, but leaves only, and said unto it, Let no fruit grow on thee henceforward for ever. And presently the fig tree withered away. And when the disciples saw it, they marveled, saying, How soon is the fig tree withered away!"

(Mt 21:19-20)

When we ask God to bring increase in any area, He arranges an opportunity to obey a time-sensitive instruction.

When we ask God for anything at a greater level than what we currently possess (money, anointing, wisdom, etc.), He shows us a small glimpse into "the new room" of His blessing we are seeking to enter.

Just as we're beginning to swell with excitement at what we think we're about to posses, He closes the door and hands us a key called an instruction.

Our reaction to that time sensitive instruction decides whether we enter into the new room!

Breaking The Back Of Poverty

I'll never forget it.

While sitting in the presence of God in a phenomenal conference, the Holy Spirit nudged me to plant a special Seed of $1000 into the vision of the house.

I had learned some years before something happens when I Sow at a $1000 level that does not occur at other levels. I have learned (and witnessed this in the lives of countless others who have planted $1000 Seeds into our vision) that when a Seed of $1000 is planted, the harvests God brings are overwhelming!

(If God ever impresses you to Sow a $1000 Seed, count off 90 days and watch what God does!)

I had prepared my Seed and was waiting for the ushers to serve me when the man of God went back to the pulpit and said these words, "The Holy Spirit has just shown me there are five people in this room He will speak to about Sowing a second Seed of $1000."

Instantly, the Holy Spirit gave me an "inner knowing". . . I was to be one of the five. My heart began to race as I explained to the Lord I had just written a check for $1000 and had not even placed it in the offering plate yet. (Maybe I'm not spiritual, but I like seeing a harvest on the last Seed I've planted before I Sow again.)

Sowing the first $1000 had not been hard. The second was much more difficult to obey.

I have learned and am learning that God never speaks to me about what's in my hand unless He's looking at what's in His.

Nothing leaves Heaven until something leaves the earth.

I planted both Seeds that day and stood up to leave the building for the dinner break. I was alone and no one but the Holy Spirit knew what I had sown. Before arriving at my car, someone called my name. I turned as a woman thrust an envelope into my hand and walked way. I opened it in my car. . . It was a check for $1000! I was thrilled. . . until I realized this couldn't be my harvest.

I had simply been given my Seed back!

I reminded the Lord I had obeyed Him, and according to His Word, I had a right to a harvest. Jesus promised a 100 fold return.
(Mk 10:28-30)

It Happened In 72 Hours.

During this season of our ministry, we were on daily radio nationwide. Our most expensive station was in New York. The air time was over $200 per broadcast.

The phone rang in our ministry office. It was that New Yok radio station. They explained they had been listening to my broadcast. It was new and refreshing, and they were excited over its content. They went on to explain, "Every once in a while, we like to do something nice for our broadcasters. Your invoice this month of $4,400 has come to our attention. We've decided to mark that invoice, "Paid in full!"

In less than 72 hours, I had received $5,400, and that was just the beginning of my harvest!

One of the *Master Rewards of Sitting in God's Presence* is His passion to promote you is unlocked. . . unleashed.

What if I had kept the $2000? There's not a doubt in my mind, the radio station would have billed us for the $4400, and all of the harvests I experienced from that Seed would have never entered my future.

God promotes those who Sow in His presence!

God's promotions are not based on age, income or education level. God's promotions are based on obedience to His last time sensitive instruction.

Have you obeyed the last instruction He gave you? If not, go back and submit to His voice.

Remember the promise of Jeremiah 29:11-14a (NKJV): "For I know the thoughts that I think toward you, says the Lord, thoughts of peace and not of evil, to give you a future and a hope. Then you will call upon Me and go and pray to Me, and I will listen to you. And you will seek Me and find Me, when you search for Me with all your heart. I will be found by you, says the Lord..."

As Dr. Mike Murdock says, *Your future has a price. . . called an instruction.*

When you enter His presence daily, His instructions will quickly follow.

God promotes those who obey Him.

God rewards those who sit at His feet.

God brings a harvest!

Divine Promotion. . . It's one of the *Master Rewards For Sitting Daily In The Presence Of God.*

Have You Invited
CHRIST INTO YOUR LIFE?

The Bible says, "All have sinned and come short of the glory of God."
(Romans 3:23)

Sin is breaking God's law—breaking His commandments.

Have you ever lied, lusted or disobeyed your parents?

Man's standard is very different from God's. Consider the following verse from Scripture:

"For whoever keeps the whole law and yet stumbles at just one point is guilty of breaking all of it."
(James 2:10 NIV)

No matter how hard we try, we cannot erase our past sins against God.

The good news is, Jesus promised, *"Whoever comes to me, I will not cast out."*

(John 6:7)

Will you turn from sin and ask Jesus Christ into your life right now?

Pray this prayer:

"Jesus, I've known right from wrong all my life. I have chosen wrong. I have sinned. I need a Savior. I repent and turn from a life of disobeying you. I invite you to come into my life and forgive me of all my sins. I confess with my mouth that Jesus Christ is my Lord and Savior. Fill me with your Spirit. I will read your Word daily and obey what I read. In Jesus' Name, Amen."

If you have prayed this prayer and truly desire to learn more about being saved and submitting every area of your life to Christ, please write me so I can send you information that will teach you what to do next and how to follow Him.

Attention: Mike Smalley
Worldreach Ministries
P.O. Box 99
Rockwall, TX 75087
www.mikesmalley.com

About
MIKE SMALLEY

Called to preach at age 14, Mike Smalley has a burden to help people. Mike is the founder of Worldreach Ministries near Dallas, Texas, which plants churches and conducts evangelistic crusades worldwide, in addition to training Christians to fulfill their life assignment. Mike has traveled to over 20 nations and has started numerous churches throughout various parts of Africa. His ministry crosses denominational lines and boundaries to take the Gospel where it is needed most.

Mike Smalley has also authored the books:

- The Young Evangelist's Handbook
- 7 Lies Christians Believe About the Lost
- Saved Soul...Wasted Life:
  Life Lessons from the Thief Next to Jesus

- How to Jumpstart Your Prayer Life

If you would like more information about Mike Smalley and Worldreach Ministries and its other ministry resources, or to invite Mike to speak in your area, write to:

Worldreach Ministries
P.O. Box 99
Rockwall, TX 75087
Or, call:
(972)771-3339
Or, you can visit Mike on the web:
www.mikesmalley.com

PURSUING GOD

These powerful teaching articles from Mike Smalley are sent
out once each month – free of charge. You can be added to the
growing list of readers and receive these challenging articles on a
regular basis. Simply send your request to:

Worldreach Ministries
P.O. Box 99
Rockwall, TX 75087
Or Call:
(972)771-3339
Or visit us online at:
www.mikesmalley.com